Margeau Chapeau

A New Perspective on Classic Knit Hats

Margeau Soboti

Dover Publications, Inc.
Mineola, New York

INTRODUCTION

As the colder weather approaches, I am always excited to knit hats! I love the ability to use my favorite thick wools to create something really special. A hat is one of those garments where you can incorporate intricate designs, but not spend endless hours knitting it. You can add special knitting techniques, add textured patterns or different color creations to design a wearable garment. I love adding vibrant colors and various textures to my wardrobe. Hats are wonderful and thoughtful holiday gifts and are the perfect portable project!

In addition to being perfect on-the-go projects; hats are also worked in the round! I love knitting in the round! This technique eliminates the need for seaming and working on wrong side rows. Most of the designs are worked from the bottom up on circular needles.

Every design is unique; some are easy and some are for experienced knitters. Cables, Fair Isle, and Brioche stitch are some fun techniques that you can find in this book.

So heat up the kettle, fix yourself a cup of tea, and work up one of these cozy and modern hats!

Copyright

Copyright © 2016 by Margeau Soboti
All rights reserved.

Bibliographical Note

Margeau Chapeau: A New Perspective on Classic Knit Hats is a new work, first published by Dover Publications, Inc., in 2016.

International Standard Book Number
ISBN-13: 978-0-486-80312-8
ISBN-10: 0-486-80312-0

Manufactured in the United States by RR Donnelley
80312001   2016
www.doverpublications.com

CONTENTS

Optical

SKILL LEVEL: INTERMEDIATE

Sized for Women.

YARN

Creative Focus Worsted by Rowan, 3½oz/100g, 220yd/200m
(75% wool, 25% alpaca)
* One ball of each in #01660 Marine (A) and #00401 Nickel (B)

NEEDLES

* Sizes 6 and 7 (4 and 4.5mm) circular needles, 16"/40cm long *or size to obtain the gauge*
* Set of 4 size 7 (4.5mm) double-pointed needles (dpns)

ADDITIONAL MATERIALS

* Stitch markers

MEASUREMENTS

Brim circumference: 18"/45.5cm
Length: 10"/25.5cm

GAUGE

26 sts and 24 rnds = 4"/10cm over colorwork pat with larger needle.
Take time to check your gauge.

HAT

With A and smaller needle, cast on 118 sts. Join, being careful not to twist sts, and place marker (pm) for beg of rnd.

Next rnd: *K1, p1; rep from * around.

Rep last rnd for k1, p1 rib until piece measures 2"/5cm from beg.

Knit 1 rnd, inc 8 sts evenly across rnd—126 sts. Change to larger needle.

Beg color pat

Rnds 1 and 2: *With A, k1, with B, k1; rep from * around.

Rnds 3 and 4: *With B, k1, with A, k1; rep from * around.

Rep rnds 1–4 until piece measures 7"/18cm from beg, ending with rnd 1.

Next rnd: [Work 7 sts in pat as established, pm] 17 times around, work in pat to end.

Shape crown

Notes: Change to dpns when there are too few sts to fit on circular needle. Maintain continuity of color pat in between each decrease.

Next (dec) rnd: [Work to 2 sts before next marker, k2tog with A, sl marker, work to 2 sts before next marker, k2tog with B] 9 times around—18 sts dec'd.

Next rnd: Work even in colors as they appear.

Rep last 2 rnds 4 times more—36 sts.

Next (dec) rnd: [K2tog with A, k2tog with B] 9 times—18 sts.

Cut yarn, leaving a long tail. Thread tail through rem sts to close.

FINISHING

With A, make 4"/10cm pompom and attach to top of hat.

Twist Turban

SKILL LEVEL: EASY

Sized for Women.

YARN

Cocoon by Rowan, 3½oz/100g skein, 126yd/115m (80% wool, 20% mohair)

∗ One skein in #00836 Moon

NEEDLES

∗ Size 8 (5mm) needles *or size to obtain the gauge*

∗ One size 8 (5mm) double-pointed needle (dpn)

ADDITIONAL MATERIALS

∗ Size H-8 (5mm) crochet hook and waste yarn
  (for provisional cast-on)

∗ Yarn needle

MEASUREMENTS

Circumference: 19"/48cm

Length: 3½"/9cm

GAUGE

18 sts and 23 rows = 4"/10cm over St st with size 8 (5mm) needles.
Take time to check your gauge.

PROVISIONAL CAST-ON
With waste yarn and crochet hook, make a slipknot and chain 2 stitches more than required to cast on, fasten off. With needles and working yarn, pick up required number of cast on stitches through the back loops of chain. When instructed, undo slipknot and carefully unravel the waste yarn, placing the released knit stitches on a needle.

KITCHENER STITCH
Hold stitches on knitting needles with WS together. Working with tail of yarn threaded through yarn needle, thread the yarn through first stitch on front needle as if to purl and leave it on the needle. *Thread the yarn through the first stitch on the back needle as if to purl and slip it off the needle. Thread the yarn through the next st on the back needle as if to knit and leave it on the needle. Thread the yarn through the first stitch on the front needle as if to knit and slip it off the needle. Thread the yarn through the next stitch on the front needle as if to purl and leave it on the needle. Rep from * until all stitches have been grafted.

NOTE
Piece is worked back and forth in one strip, which is divided in 2 parts, then are crossed and joined to create the twist. The provisional cast-on is removed and grafted to the opposite end to form a tube.

TURBAN
Cast on 22 sts using provisional cast-on method.

Next row (WS): [K1, p4] twice, k2, [p4, k1] twice.

Next row (RS): [P1, k4] twice, p2, [k4, p1] twice.

Rep last 2 rows for rib pat until piece measures 8"/10cm from beg, ending with WS row.

Divide for twist
Next row (RS): Work in pat over first 11 sts. Turn, leaving rem sts on needle to hold.

Cont in pat on the first 11 sts until piece measures 10¼"/26cm from beg, ending with WS row. Cut yarn and place sts on dpn to hold. Join yarn to rem 11 sts, and work in pat as established until piece measures same as other side.

Join twist

Cross one side over the other for twist. Join new strand of yarn and work in rib pat over 22 sts until piece measures 8"/20.5cm from joining, ending with RS row. Do *not* bind off. Cut yarn, leaving a long tail.

FINISHING

Carefully undo provisional cast-on, placing sts on dpn and graft ends tog using Kitchener stitch. Block lightly.

New Yorker Watch Cap

SKILL LEVEL: EASY
Sized for Women and (Men).

YARN

Wool-Ease by Lion Brand, 3oz/85g, 197yd/180m (80% acrylic, 20% wool)
∗ One skein in #123 Seaspray or #159 Mustard or #152 Oxford Grey

NEEDLES

∗ Size 5 (3.75mm) circular needle, 16"/40cm long *or size to obtain the gauge*
∗ Set of 4 size 5 (3.75mm) double-pointed needles (dpns)

ADDITIONAL MATERIALS

∗ Stitch marker

MEASUREMENTS

Circumference: 18 (20)"/45.5 (51)cm
Length: 8"/20.5cm with brim folded

GAUGE

22 sts and 28 rnds = 4"/10cm over St st with size 5 (3.75mm) needle.
Take time to check your gauge.

HAT

Cast on 100 (110) sts. Join, being careful not to twist sts, and place marker (pm) for beg of rnd.

Next rnd: *K1, p1; rep from * around.

Rep last rnd until piece measures 5"/12.5cm from beg. Work in St st (k every rnd) until piece measures 8"/20.5cm from beg.

Shape crown

Note: Change to dpns when there are too few sts to fit on circular needle.

Next (dec) rnd: [K8, k2tog] 10 (11) times—90 (99) sts.

Next rnd: Knit.

Next (dec) rnd: [K7, k2tog] 10 (11) times—80 (88) sts.

Next rnd: Knit.

Next (dec) rnd: [K6, k2tog] 10 (11) times—70 (77) sts.

Next rnd: Knit.

Next (dec) rnd: [K5, k2tog] 10 (11) times—60 (66) sts.

Next rnd: Knit.

Next (dec) rnd: [K4, k2tog] 10 (11) times—50 (55) sts.

Next rnd: Knit.

Next (dec) rnd: [K3, k2tog] 10 (11) times—40 (44) sts.

Next rnd: Knit.

Next (dec) rnd: [K2, k2tog] 10 (11) times—30 (33) sts.

Next rnd: Knit.

Next (dec) rnd: [K1, k2tog] 10 (11) times—20 (22) sts.

Next rnd: Knit.

Next (dec) rnd: [K2tog] 10 (11) times—10 (11) sts.

Cut yarn, leaving a long tail. Thread tail through rem sts to close.

Fold brim 2½"/6.5cm to RS to wear.

Brioche Beanie

SKILL LEVEL: INTERMEDIATE
Sized for Women.

YARN
Rialto Chunky by Debbie Bliss, 1¾oz/50g, 66yd/60m (100% extrafine superwash merino wool)
* Three balls in #43023 Olive

NEEDLES
* Sizes 7 and 9 (4.5 and 5.5mm) needles *or size to obtain the gauge*

MEASUREMENTS
Circumference: 18"/45.5cm
Length: 10"/25.5cm

GAUGE
19 sts and 18 rows = 4"/10cm over brioche st with larger needles.
Take time to check your gauge.

BRIOCHE STITCH
(Over an even number of sts)
Row 1: *Yo, sl 1, k2tog; rep from * to end of row.

Row 2: *Yo, sl 1, k2tog (sl stitch and yo from previous row); rep from * to end of row.

Rep row 2 for brioche st.

NOTE
Hat is worked flat, in rows, and seamed when knitting is complete.

HAT

With smaller needles, cast on 84 sts.

Next row (WS): *K1, p1; rep from * to end of row.

Rep last row until piece measures 1½"/4cm from beg, ending with WS row. Change to larger needles.

Beg brioche st

Work in brioche st until piece measures 8¼"/21cm from beg, ending with WS row.

Shape crown

Next (dec) row (RS): *[Yo, sl 1, k2tog] 3 times, sl 1, k2tog; rep from * 6 times more—77 sts.

Next row (WS): *Sl 1 wyif, k1, [yo, sl 1, k2tog] 3 times; rep from * 6 times more.

Next (dec) row: *[Yo, sl 1, k2tog] 3 times, k2tog; rep from * 6 times more—70 sts.

Next (dec) row: *P1, sl 1 wyif, k2tog, [yo, sl 1, k2tog] twice; rep from * 6 times more—63 sts.

Next (dec) row: *[Yo, sl 1, k2tog] twice, sl 1, k2tog; rep from * 6 times more—56 sts.

Next row: *Sl 1 wyif, k1, [yo, sl 1, k2tog] twice; rep from * 6 times more.

Next (dec) row: *[Yo, sl 1, k2tog] twice, k2tog; rep from * 6 times more—49 sts.

Next (dec) row: *P1, sl 1 wyif, k2tog, yo, sl 1, k2tog; rep from * 6 times more—42 sts.

Next (dec) row: *Yo, sl 1, k2tog, sl 1, k2tog; rep from * 6 times more—35 sts.

Next row: *Sl 1 wyif, k1, yo, sl 1, k2tog; rep from * 6 times more.

Next (dec) row: *Yo, sl 1, k2tog, k2tog; rep from * 6 times more—28 sts.

Next (dec) row: *P1, sl 1 wyif, k1; rep from * 6 times more—21 sts.

Next (dec) row: *Sl 1, k2tog; rep from * 6 times more—14 sts.

Next (dec) row: *P2tog; rep from * 6 times more—7 sts.

Cut yarn, leaving a long tail. With RS facing, thread tail through rem sts. Use tail to sew seam using a half st each side.

Very Berry Cabler

SKILL LEVEL: EASY
Sized for Women.

YARN

Big Wool by Rowan, 3½oz/100g, 87yd/80m (100% wool)
* Two balls in #079 Pantomime

NEEDLES

* Sizes 11 and 13 (8 and 9mm) circular needles, 16"/40cm long *or size to obtain the gauge*
* Set of 4 size 13 (9mm) double-pointed needles (dpns)

ADDITIONAL MATERIALS

* Cable needle (cn)
* Stitch marker

MEASUREMENTS

Circumference: 18"/45.5cm
Length: 8"/20.5cm

GAUGE

10 sts and 14 rows = 4"/10cm over St st with larger needle.
14 sts and 14 rows = 4"/10cm over plait cable pat with larger needle.
Take time to check your gauge.

27

PLAIT CABLE PATTERN
(Multiple of 9 sts)

Rnds 1 and 3: *P3, k6; rep from * around.

Rnd 2: *P3, RC, k2; rep from * around.

Rnd 4: *P3, k2, LC; rep from * around.

Rep rnds 1–4 for plait cable pat.

STITCH GLOSSARY
RC: Sl 2 sts to cn and hold to *back*, k2, k2 from cn.
LC: Sl 2 sts to cn and hold to *front*, k2, k2 from cn.

HAT
With smaller needle, cast on 64 sts. Join, being careful not to twist sts, and place marker (pm) for beg of rnd.

Next rnd: *K1, p1; rep from * around.

Rep last rnd until piece measures 2¼"/5.5cm from beg, k2tog at end of last rnd—63 sts. Change to larger needle.

Beg plait cable pat
Rnd 1: Work 9-st rep of plait cable pat 7 times around.

Cont in plait cable pat through rnd 4. Rep rnds 1–4 three times more.

Shape crown
Note: Change to dpns when there are too few sts to fit on circular needle.

Next (dec) rnd: [P2tog, p1, k4, k2tog] 7 times—49 sts.

Next rnd: [P2, RC, k1] 7 times.

Next (dec) rnd: [P2tog, k2tog, k3] 7 times—35 sts.

Next rnd: [P1, LC] 7 times.

Next (dec) rnd: [P1, k2tog, k2tog] 7 times—21 sts.

Next rnd: [P1, k2] 7 times.

Next (dec) rnd: [P1, k2tog] 7 times—14 sts.

Cut yarn, leaving a long tail. Thread tail through rem sts to close.

FINISHING
Make 4"/10cm pompom and attach to top of hat.

Avalanche

SKILL LEVEL: EASY
Sized for Women.

YARN

LB Collection Wool Yarn by Lion Brand, 7oz/200g, 22yd/20m (100% wool)

* Two hanks in Cream

NEEDLES

* Set of 4 size 15 (10mm) double-pointed needles (dpns) *or size to obtain the gauge*

ADDITIONAL MATERIALS

* Stitch marker

MEASUREMENTS

Circumference: 20"/51cm
Length: 9"/23cm

GAUGE
5 sts and 6 rnds = 4"/10cm over St st with size 15 (10mm) needles.
Take time to check your gauge.

HAT
Cast on 25 sts. Join, being careful not to twist sts, and place marker (pm) for beg of rnd. Work in St st (k every rnd), for 11 rnds.

Shape crown
Next (dec) rnd: *K3, k2tog; rep from * around—20 sts.

Next (dec) rnd: *K2, k2tog; rep from * around—15 sts.

Next (dec) rnd: *K1, k2tog; rep from * around—10 sts.

Next (dec) rnd: *K2tog; rep from * around—5 sts.

Cut yarn, leaving a long tail. Thread tail through rem sts to close.

FINISHING
Make 4"/10cm pompom and attach to top of hat.

Marled Bomber and Mitts

SKILL LEVEL: EASY

Sized for Women.

YARN

Extra by Blue Sky Alpacas, 5¼oz/150g, 218yd/199m (55% baby alpaca, 45% fine merino)
* One hank of each in #3510 Butter Cream (A) and #3514 Marsh (B)

NEEDLES

* Size 11 (8mm) circular needle, 16"/40cm long *or size to obtain the gauge*
* Set of 4 size 11 (8mm) double-pointed needles (dpns)

ADDITIONAL MATERIALS

* Stitch holders
* Size J-10 (6mm) crochet hook

MEASUREMENTS

Circumference of brim: 18"/45.5cm
Length (excluding earflaps and pompom): 7"/18cm

GAUGE

12 sts and 16 rnds = 4"/10cm over St st with size 11 (8mm) needle and 1 strand each of A and B held tog.
Take time to check your gauge.

STITCH GLOSSARY

M1R: With left-hand needle, insert tip from back to front under strand between last stitch knit and next stitch on left-hand needle, and bring up a loop. Knit into *front* of this loop—1 stitch increased.

M1L: With left-hand needle, insert tip from front to back under strand between last stitch knit and next stitch on left-hand needle, and bring up a loop. Knit into *back* of this loop—1 stitch increased.

Sc2tog: Insert hook in stitch, yarn over and pull up a loop, insert hook in next stitch and pull up a loop, 3 loops on hook, yarn over and pull through all 3 loops on hook—1 stitch decreased.

EARFLAP

(Make 2)

With 1 strand each of A and B held tog, cast on 3 sts. Purl 1 row.

Next (inc) row (RS): K1, M1R, k to last st, M1L, k1—2 sts inc'd.

Purl 1 row.

Rep last 2 rows twice more—9 sts.

Knit 1 row, purl 1 row.

Next (inc) row (RS): K1, M1R, k to last st, M1L, k1—11 sts.

Work 3 rows even in St st (k on RS, p on WS).

Place on stitch holder.

HAT

With 1 strand each of A and B held tog, k11 from first earflap holder, cast on 18 sts for front of hat, k11 from 2nd earflap holder, cast on 14 sts for back of hat—54 sts.

Join and place marker for beg of rnd.

Work in St st (k every rnd) until piece measures 6"/15cm from beg.

Shape crown

Note: Change to dpns when there are too few sts to fit on circular needle.

Next (dec) rnd: [K4, k2tog] 9 times—45 sts.

Knit 1 rnd.

Next (dec) rnd: [K3, k2tog] 9 times—36 sts.

Knit 1 rnd.

Next (dec) rnd [K2, k2tog] 9 times—27 sts.

Knit 1 rnd.

Next (dec) rnd: [K1, k2tog] 9 times—18 sts.

Knit 1 rnd.

Next (dec) rnd: [K2tog] 9 times—9 sts.

Knit 1 rnd.

Cut yarn, leaving a long tail. Thread tail through rem sts to close.

FINISHING

With RS facing, crochet hook and 1 strand each of A and B held tog, work 1 rnd of single crochet (sc) around brim and earflaps. Fasten off.

Tassels

With RS facing, crochet hook and 1 strand each of A and B held tog, sc 5 sts along bottom of earflap. Ch 1, turn.

Next row: Sc2tog, sc, sc2tog—3 sc. Ch 1, turn.

Next row: Sc 1, sc2tog—2 sc. Ch 1, turn.

Next row: Sc2tog—1 sc.

Fasten off last st, leaving a tail 18"/45.5cm long.

Holding 1 strand each of A and B tog, cut 2 more lengths 18"/45.5cm long. Braid the 3 lengths together for 8"/20.5cm. Tie knot at bottom of braid, trim tassel to 3"/6.5cm below knot.

With A and B held tog, make a 4"/10cm pompom, attach to top of hat.

MITTS

Note: Mitts are worked in rows. Do *not* join.
With 1 strand each of A and B held tog, cast on 21 sts. Work in St st (k on RS, p on WS) until piece measures 7"/18cm from beg, ending with WS row. Bind off.

FINISHING

Fold mitt in half lengthwise and sew seam 1½"/4cm down from top and 3"/6.5cm up from bottom, leaving opening for thumb.

Fisherman's Beanie

SKILL LEVEL: INTERMEDIATE

Sized for Women.

YARN

Alpaca Chunky by Rowan, 3½oz/100g, 77yd/70m (98% alpaca, 2% polyamide)
* Two balls in #072 Wren

NEEDLES

* Size 11 (8mm) circular needle, 16"/40cm long *or size to obtain the gauge*
* Set of 4 size 11 (8mm) double-pointed needles (dpns)

ADDITIONAL MATERIALS

* Stitch marker

MEASUREMENTS

Circumference (unstretched): 18"/45.5cm
Length with brim folded: 8"/20.5cm

GAUGE

12½ sts and 20 rows = 4"/10cm over Fisherman's Rib with size 11 (8mm) needle.
Take time to check your gauge.

FISHERMAN'S RIB

(Worked in rows, over an odd number of sts)
Row 1 (RS): *K1 into the row below, p1; rep from * to last st, k1 into the row below.

Row 2 (WS): *K1, p1; rep from * to last st, k1.

Rep rows 1 and 2 for fisherman's rib in rows.

FISHERMAN'S RIB

(Worked in the rnd, over an even number of sts)
Rnd 1: *K1 into the row below, p1; rep from * around.

Rnd 2: *K1, p1; rep from * around.

Rep rnds 1 and 2 for fisherman's rib in the rnd.

NOTE

Brim of hat is worked flat, in rows, and then joined to work remainder of hat in the round. Brim is seamed when knitting is complete.

HAT

Cast on 57 sts. Beg with a WS row 2, work in fisherman's rib until piece measures 2½"/6.5cm from beg, ending with RS row.

Next (dec) row: K2tog, *p1, k1; rep from * to end—56 sts.

Join and place marker for beg of rnd. Cont in fisherman's rib as established until piece measures 9"/23cm from beg, ending with rnd 1.

Shape crown

Note: Change to dpns when there are too few sts to fit on circular needle.

Next (dec) rnd: [Ssk, work 6 sts in pat] 7 times—49 sts.

Next rnd: Work even in pat.

Next (dec) rnd: [Ssk, work 5 sts in pat] 7 times—42 sts.

Next rnd: Work even in pat.

Next (dec) rnd: [Ssk, work 4 sts in pat] 7 times—35 sts.

Next rnd: Work even in pat.

Next (dec) rnd: [Ssk, work 3 sts in pat] 7 times—28 sts.

Next rnd: Work even in pat.

Next (dec) rnd: [Ssk, work 2 sts in pat] 7 times—21 sts.

Next rnd: Work even in pat.

Next (dec) rnd: [Ssk, work 1 st in pat] 7 times—14 sts.

Next (dec) rnd: [Ssk] 7 times—7 sts.

Cut yarn, leaving a long tail. Thread tail through rem sts to close.

Fold brim 2½"/6.5cm to RS and sew back seam with RS facing.

Zig-Zag Colorwork

SKILL LEVEL: INTERMEDIATE

Sized for Women.

YARN

Roma by Debbie Bliss, 3½oz/100g, 87yd/80m (70% wool, 30% alpaca)
⋆ One ball of each in #05 Taupe (A) and #04 Chocolate (B)

NEEDLES

⋆ Sizes 11 and 13 (8 and 9mm) circular needles, 16"/40cm long *or size to obtain the gauge*
⋆ Set of 4 size 13 (9mm) double-pointed needles (dpns)

ADDITIONAL MATERIALS

⋆ Stitch marker

MEASUREMENTS

Circumference: 18"/45.5cm
Length: 9"/23cm

GAUGE

12 sts and 12 rnds = 4"/10cm over St st with larger needle.
Take time to check your gauge.

STITCH GLOSSARY

K3tog: Knit 3 sts together to decrease 2 sts.

HAT

With A and smaller needle, cast on 54 sts. Join, being careful not to twist sts, and place marker (pm) for beg of rnd.

Next rnd: *K1, p1; rep from * around.

Rep last rnd until piece measures 2"/5cm from beg. Change to larger needle.

Beg colorwork chart

Note: Work remainder of hat in St st (k every rnd) while foll chart for color pat.

Next rnd: Work 18-st rep 3 times around.

Cont to foll chart in this way through rnd 15.

Shape crown

Note: Change to dpns when there are too few sts to fit on circular needle.

Next (dec) rnd: [K1 B, k1 A, k1 B, k1 A, k1 B, k1 A, with B, k3tog, k1 A, k1 B, k1 A, k1 B, k1 A, k1 B, with A, k3tog] 3 times—42 sts.

Next rnd: Work even in colors as they appear.

Next (dec) rnd: [K1 A, k1 B, k1 A, k1 B, with A, k3tog, k1 B, k1 A, k1 B, k1 A, with B, k3tog] 3 times—30 sts.

Next rnd: Work even in colors as they appear.

Next (dec) rnd: [K1 B, k1 A, with B, k3tog, k1 B, k1 A, with B, k3tog] 3 times—18 sts.

Next rnd: Work even in colors as they appear.

Next (dec) rnd: [With A, k3tog, with B, k3tog] 3 times—6 sts.

Cut yarn, leaving a long tail. Thread tail through rem sts to close.

FINISHING

With A and B, make 4"/10cm pompom and attach to top of hat.

COLORWORK CHART

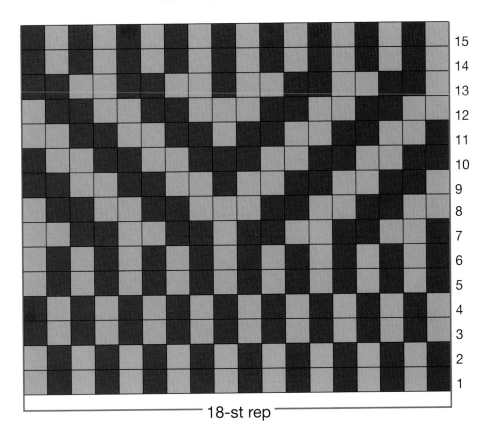

15
14
13
12
11
10
9
8
7
6
5
4
3
2
1

— 18-st rep —

Key

Taupe 05 (A)

Chocolate 04 (B)

Charlie Chevron

SKILL LEVEL: INTERMEDIATE
Sized for Women.

YARN

LB Collection Cashmere by Lion Brand, .88oz/25g, 82yd/75m
(100% cashmere)
* Three balls in #134 Terracotta

NEEDLES

* Size 5 (3.75mm) circular needle, 16"/40cm long *or size to obtain the gauge*
* Set of 4 size 5 (3.75mm) double-pointed needles (dpns)

MEASUREMENTS

Circumference: 18"/45.5cm
Length: 10"/25.5cm

GAUGE

24 sts and 36 rows = 4"/10cm over St st with size 5 (3.75mm) needle.
Take time to check your gauge.

CHEVRON PATTERN

(Multiple of 8 sts)
Rnds 1 and 2: *P1, k7; rep from * around.

Rnds 3 and 4: *P2, k5, p1; rep from * around.

Rnds 5 and 6: *P3, k3, p2; rep from * around.

Rnds 7 and 8: *P4, k1, p3; rep from * around.

Rnds 9 and 10: *K1, p7; rep from * around.

Rnds 11 and 12: *K2, p5, k1; rep from * around.

Rnds 13 and 14: *K3, p3, k2; rep from * around.

Rnds 15 and 16: *K4, p1, k3; rep from * around.

Rep rnds 1–16 for chevron pat.

HAT

Cast on 108 sts. Join, being careful not to twist sts, and place marker (pm) for beg of rnd.

Next rnd: *K1, p1; rep from * around.

Rep last rnd for k1, p1 rib until piece measures 1"/2.5cm from beg.

Next rnd: Knit, inc 4 sts evenly across next row—112 sts.

Work in St st (k every rnd) until piece measures 1½"/4cm from beg.

Beg chevron pat

Note: Chevron pat can be worked using written instructions *or* chart. Note that each charted rnd is worked twice.

Next rnd: Work 8-st rep of chevron pat 14 times around.

Cont to work chevron pat in this way through rnd 16. Rep rnds 1–16 three times more.

Next rnd: Knit, dec 2 sts evenly—110 sts.

Shape crown

Note: Change to dpns when there are too few sts to fit on circular needle.

Next (dec) rnd: [K9, k2tog] 10 times—100 sts.

Next rnd: Knit.

Next (dec) rnd: [K8, k2tog] 10 times—90 sts.

Next rnd: Knit.

CHEVRON PATTERN

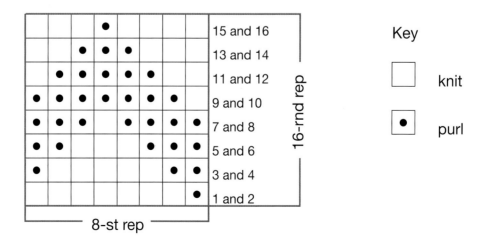

Next (dec) rnd: [K7, k2tog] 10 times—80 sts.

Next rnd: Knit.

Next (dec) rnd: [K6, k2tog] 10 times—70 sts.

Next rnd: Knit.

Next (dec) rnd: [K5, k2tog] 10 times—60 sts.

Next rnd: Knit.

Next (dec) rnd: [K4, k2tog] 10 times—50 sts.

Next rnd: Knit.

Next (dec) rnd: [K3, k2tog] 10 times—40 sts.

Next rnd: Knit.

Next (dec) rnd: [K2, k2tog] 10 times—30 sts.

Next rnd: Knit.

Next (dec) rnd: [K1, k2tog] 10 times—20 sts.

Next rnd: Knit.

Next (dec) rnd: [K2tog] 10 times—10 sts.

Cut yarn, leaving a long tail. Thread tail through rem sts to close.

FINISHING
Steam block to finished measurements.

Serpentine
Cabled

SKILL LEVEL: INTERMEDIATE
Sized for Women.

YARN

Rialto Chunky by Debbie Bliss, 1¾oz/50g, 66yd/60m
(100% extrafine superwash merino wool)
* Three balls in #22 Storm

NEEDLES

* Sizes 7 and 9 (4.5 and 5.5mm) circular needles, 16"/40cm long *or
  size to obtain the gauge*
* Set of 4 size 7 (4.5mm) double-pointed needles (dpns)

ADDITIONAL MATERIALS

* Cable needle (cn)
* Stitch marker

MEASUREMENTS

Circumference: 19¼"/49cm
Length: 8"/20.5cm

GAUGE

20 sts and 21 rnds = 4"/10cm over Serpentine Cables with
larger needles.
Take time to check your gauge.

STITCH GLOSSARY

K3tog: Knit 3 sts together to decrease 2 sts.

LPC: Sl 2 sts to cn and hold to *front*, p1, k2 from cn.

RPC: Sl 1 st to cn and hold to *back*, k2, p1 from cn.

LC: Sl 2 sts to cn and hold to *front*, k2, k2 from cn.

SERPENTINE CABLE

(over 20 sts)

Rnds 1 and 2: P3, [k2, p2] 4 times, p1.

Rnd 3: P3, [LPC, RPC, p2] twice, p1.

Rnd 4 and all even rnds: K the knit sts and p the purl sts.

Rnd 5: P4, [LC, p4] twice.

Rnd 7: P3, [RPC, LPC, p2] twice, p1.

Rnd 9: P2, [RPC, p2, LPC] twice, p2.

Rnd 11: P1, RPC, p4, LC, p4, LPC, p1.

Rnd 13: RPC, p4, RPC, LPC, p4, LPC.

Rnd 15: K the knit sts and p the purl sts.

Rnd 17: LPC, p4, LPC, RPC, p4, RPC.

Rnd 19: P1, LPC, p4, LC, p4, RPC, p1.

Rnd 21: P2, [LPC, p2, RPC] twice, p2.

Rnd 23: P3, [LPC, RPC, p2] twice, p1.

Rnd 25: P4, [LC, p4] twice.

Rnd 27: P3, [RPC, LPC, p2] twice, p1.

Rnd 29: K the knit sts and p the purl sts.

Rnds 1–29 make up serpentine cable.

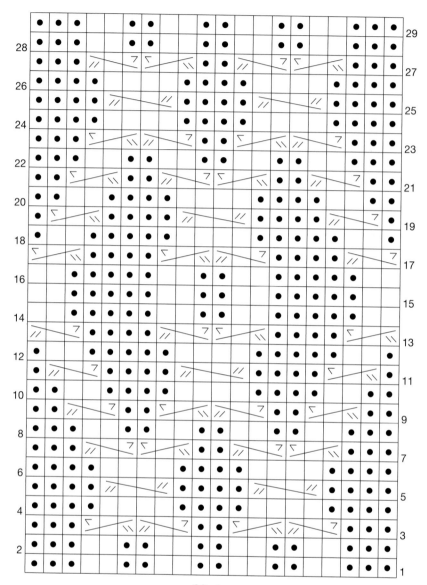

20 sts

TRAVELING CABLE

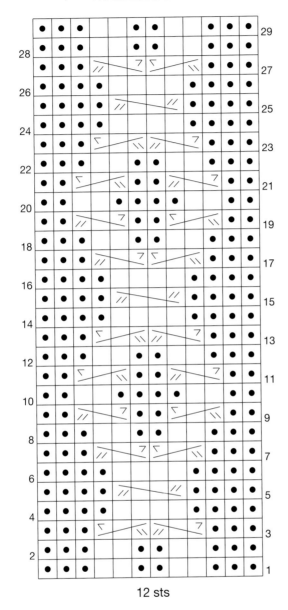

12 sts

Key

☐ knit

● purl

LPC

RPC

LC

TRAVELING CABLE

(over 6 sts)

Rnds 1 and 2: P3, k2, p2, k2, p3.

Rnd 3: P3, LPC, RPC, p3.

Rnd 4 and all even rnds: K the knit sts and p the purl sts.

Rnd 5: P4, LC, p4.

Rnd 7: P3, RPC, LPC, p3.

Rnd 9: P2, RPC, p2, LPC, p2.

Rnd 11: P2, LPC, p2, RPC, p2.

Rnd 13: P3, LPC, RPC, p3.

Rnd 15: P4, LC, p4.

Rnd 17: P3, RPC, LPC, p3.

Rnd 19: P2, RPC, p2, LPC, p2.

Rnd 21: P2, LPC, p2, RPC, p2.

Rnd 23: P3, LPC, RPC, p3.

Rnd 25: P4, LC, p4.

Rnd 27: P3, RPC, LPC, p3.

Rnd 29: K the knit sts and p the purl sts.

Rnds 1–29 make up traveling cable.

HAT

With smaller needle, cast on 96 sts. Join, being careful not to twist sts, and place marker (pm) for beg of rnd.

Next rnd: *K1, p1; rep from * around.

Rep last rnd for k1, p1 rib until piece measures 1"/2.5cm from beg. Change to larger needle.

Beg cable pats

Note: Cable pats can be worked using written instructions *or* chart.

Rnd 1: [Work 20 sts of serpentine cable, work 12 sts of traveling cable] 3 times around.

Cont to work pats in this way through rnd 29.

Shape crown

Note: Change to dpns when there are too few sts to fit on circular needle.

Next (dec) rnd: [P2tog, p1, k2, p2tog, k2, p2, k2, p2tog, k2, p3, p2tog, p1, k2, p2tog, k2, p2tog, p1] 3 times—78 sts.

Next rnd: K the knit sts and p the purl sts.

Next (dec) rnd: [P2tog, k2, p1, k2, p2tog, k2, p1, k2, p2tog, p1, p2tog, k2, k2tog, k1, p2tog] 3 times—60 sts.

Next rnd: [P1, k2, p1, k2, p1, k2, p1, k2, p3, LC, p1] 3 times.

Next (dec) rnd: [P1, k2tog, p1, k2tog, p1, k2tog, p1, k2tog, p2, k2tog, k2, ssk] 3 times—42 sts.

Next rnd: K the knit sts and p the purl sts.

Next (dec) rnd: [K2tog, p1, k1, k2tog, p1, k1, p2tog, k2tog, k2tog] 3 times—27 sts.

Next rnd: K the knit sts, p the purl sts.

Next (dec) rnd: [K2tog] 12 times, k3tog—13 sts.

Cut yarn, leaving a long tail. Thread tail through rem sts to close.

FINISHING

Make 4"/10cm pompom and attach to top of hat.

Simple Rib

SKILL LEVEL: EASY
Sized for Women.

YARN

Baby Cashmerino by Debbie Bliss, 1¾oz/50g, 137yd/125m
(55% merino wool, 33% microfiber acrylic, 12% cashmere)
★ Two balls in #64 Mink

Angel by Debbie Bliss, .88oz/25g, 220yd/201m (76% super kid mohair, 24% silk)
★ One ball in #34 Buttermilk

NEEDLES

★ Size 4 (3.5mm) circular needle, 16"/40cm long *or size to obtain the gauge*
★ Set of 4 size 4 (3.5mm) double-pointed needles (dpns)

MEASUREMENTS

Circumference: 20"/51cm
Length: 10"/25.5cm

GAUGE

28 sts and 29 rnds = 4"/10cm over k1, p1 rib with size 4 (3.5mm) needle.
Take time to check your gauge.

HAT

Cast on 140 sts. Join, being careful not to twist sts, and place marker (pm) for beg of rnd.

Next rnd: *K1, p1; rep from * around.

Rep last rnd for k1, p1 rib until piece measures 8½"/21.5cm from beg.

Shape crown

Note: Change to dpns when there are too few sts to fit on circular needle.

Next (dec) rnd: *[K1, p1] 4 times, k2tog; rep from * around—126 sts.

Next rnd: K the knit sts and p the purl sts.

Next (dec) rnd: *[K1, p1] 3 times, k1, k2tog; rep from * around—112 sts.

Next rnd: K the knit sts and p the purl sts.

Next (dec) rnd: *[K1, p1] 3 times, k2tog; rep from * around—98 sts.

Next rnd: K the knit sts and p the purl sts.

Next (dec) rnd: *[K1, p1] twice, k1, k2tog; rep from * around—84 sts.

Next rnd: K the knit sts and p the purl sts.

Next (dec) rnd: *[K1, p1] twice, k2tog; rep from * around—70 sts.

Next rnd: K the knit sts and p the purl sts.

Next (dec) rnd: *K1, p1, k1, k2tog; rep from * around—56 sts.

Next rnd: K the knit sts and p the purl sts.

Next (dec) rnd: *K1, p1, k2tog; rep from * around—42 sts.

Next rnd: K the knit sts and p the purl sts.

Next (dec) rnd: *K1, k2tog; rep from * around—28 sts.

Next rnd: Knit.

Next (dec) rn: *K2tog; rep from * around—14 sts.

Cut yarn, leaving a long tail. Thread tail through rem sts to close.

Bulky
Fair Isle

SKILL LEVEL: INTERMEDIATE

Sized for Women.

YARN

Bulky by Blue Sky Alpacas, 3½oz/100g, 45yd/41m (50% alpaca, 50% wool)
* Two skeins in #1214 Pluto (A)
* One skein in #1002 Silver Mink (B)

NEEDLES

* Size 13 and 15 (9 and 10mm) circular needles, 16"/40cm long or *size to obtain the gauge*
* Set of 4 size 15 (10mm) double-pointed needles (dpns)

MEASUREMENTS

Circumference: 19¼"/49cm
Length: 9"/23cm

GAUGE

10 sts and 11 rnds = 4"/10cm over St st with larger needle.
Take time to check your gauge.

HAT

With A and smaller needles, cast on 48 sts. Join, being careful not to twist sts, and place marker (pm) for beg of rnd.

Next rnd: *K1, p1; rep from * around.

Rep last rnd for k1, p1 rib until piece measures 2"/5cm from beg. Change to larger needle. With B, knit 1 rnd.

Beg chart

Note: Work remainder of hat in St st (k every rnd) while following chart.

Rnd 1: Work 16-st rep 3 times around.

Cont to foll chart in this way through rnd 15. Cut B. With A, work 1 rnd.

Shape crown

Note: Change to dpns when there are too few sts to fit on circular needle.

Next (dec) rnd: *K4, k2tog; rep from * around—40 sts.

Next rnd: Knit.

Next (dec) rnd: *K3, k2tog; rep from * around—32 sts.

Next rnd: Knit.

Next (dec) rnd: *K2, k2tog; rep from * around—24 sts.

Next (dec) rnd: *K1, k2tog; rep from * around—16 sts.

Next (dec) rnd: [K2tog] 8 times—8 sts.

Cut yarn, leaving a long tail. Thread tail through rem sts to close.

FINISHING

With A, make 4"/10cm pompom and attach to top of hat.

COLORWORK CHART

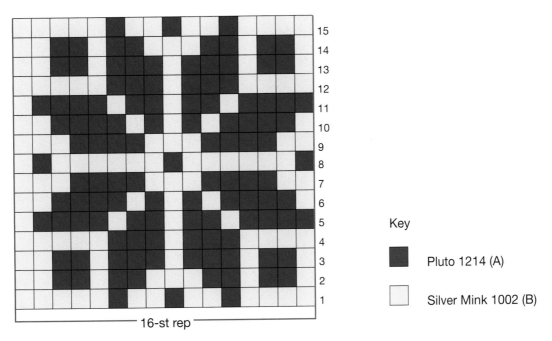

Key

Pluto 1214 (A)

Silver Mink 1002 (B)

16-st rep

Ombré Hat

SKILL LEVEL: EASY

Sized for Women.

YARN
Alpaca Colour by Rowan, 1¾oz/50g, 131yd/120m (100% alpaca)
* Two hanks of each in #139 Garnet (A) and #141 Amethyst (B)

NEEDLES
* Sizes 6 and 7 (4 and 4.5mm) circular needles, 16"/40cm long *or size to obtain the gauge*
* Set of 4 size 7 (4.5mm) double-pointed needles (dpns)

ADDTIONAL MATERIALS
* Stitch marker

MEASUREMENTS
Circumference: 18"/45.5cm
Length: 9½"/24cm

GAUGE
20 sts and 26 rnds = 4"/10cm over St st with 2 strands of yarn held together and larger needle.
Take time to check your gauge.

HAT

With 2 strands of A held tog and smaller needles, cast on 90 sts. Join, being careful not to twist sts, and place marker for beg of rnd.

Next rnd: *K1, p1; rep from * around.
Rep last rnd until piece measures 1½"/4cm from beg. Change to larger needles.

Beg ombré pat

Work in St st (k every rnd) until piece measures 3"/6.5cm from beg. Cut 1 strand A, join B. With 1 strand each of A and B held tog, cont in St st until piece measures 6"/15cm from beg. Cut A, join 2nd strand B. With 2 strands of B held tog, cont in St st until piece measures 7"/18cm from beg.

Shape crown

Note: Change to dpns when there are too few sts to fit on circular needle.

Next (dec) rnd: *K7, k2tog; rep from * around—80 sts.

Next rnd: Knit.

Next (dec) rnd: *K6, k2tog; rep from * around—70 sts.

Next rnd: Knit.

Next (dec) rnd: *K5, k2tog; rep from * around—60 sts.

Next rnd: Knit.

Next (dec) rnd: *K4, k2tog; rep from * around—50 sts.

Next rnd: Knit.

Next (dec) rnd: *K3, k2tog; rep from * around—40 sts.

Next rnd: Knit.

Next (dec) rnd: *K2, k2tog; rep from * around—30 sts.

Next rnd: Knit.

Next (dec) rnd: *K1, k2tog; rep from * around—20 sts.

Next rnd: Knit.

Next (dec) rnd: *K2tog; rep from * around—10 sts.

Cut yarn, leaving a long tail. Thread tail through rem sts to close.

List of Abbreviations

beg	Begin
ch	Chain
cn	Cable needle
cont	Continue
dec	Decrease
dpn(s)	Double-pointed needle(s)
foll	Follow
inc	Increase
k	Knit
k2tog	Knit two together
k3tog	Knit three together
LC	Left cross
LPC	Left purl cross
M1R	Make one right
M1L	Make one left
p	Purl
pat	Pattern
pm	Place marker
p2tog	Purl two together
RC	Right cross
rem	Remain/remaining
rep	Repeat
rnd(s)	Round(s)
RPC	Right purl cross
RS	Right side
sc	Single crochet
sc2tog	Single crochet two together
sl	Slip
ssk	Slip, slip, knit
st(s)	Stitch(es)
St st	Stockinette stitch
tog	Together
WS	Wrong side
wyif	With yarn in front
yo	Yarn over

CREDITS

Photographer: Melisse Dilger

Stylist Assistant: Rebecca Soboti

Model: Joanna Radow

Sample Knitters: Leslie Tiras and Donna Capolongo